BEST
Cookies
EVER

Beyond ho-hum to Oh, YUM!

Tools of the Trade

Use light-colored cookie sheets *(be sure they're cool)* and cover with parchment paper or silicone baking mats for even baking and easy clean-ups. It's best to bake one pan of cookies at a time, but if you must use both oven racks, swap and rotate the pans halfway through baking time. Cool cookies on the pan briefly before transferring to a wire rack to finish cooling.

ISBN-13: 978-1-56383-486-8
Item #7135

**Printed in the USA
by G&R Publishing Co.**

Distributed By:

507 Industrial Street
Waverly, IA 50677

www.cqbookstore.com

gifts@cqbookstore.com

 CQ Products

 CQ Products

 @cqproducts

 @cqproducts

Make Your Best Cookies Ever

Use all-purpose white flour and granulated white sugar unless recipes specify a different type. Spoon flour, sugar, and other dry ingredients into the cup, then level off *(no sifting required)*. Always pack brown sugar – it should hold the cup's shape.

Check liquid measurements at eye level, and let dairy products warm up to room temperature before using.

Use large eggs at room temperature. *(In a hurry? Set them in a bowl of warmish water.)*

Use salted or unsalted butter or stick margarine per recipe directions. To soften, let stand at room temperature a few hours, or microwave on 20% power in 20-second bursts until soft, but not mushy or melted. *(Melted butter mixes into dough much differently.)*

Use the right leavening – baking soda and baking powder aren't interchangeable. And don't omit the salt – it balances the flavors.

When is a Twix candy bar NOT a candy bar? When it's turned into a caramel-topped, chocolate-kissed shortbread cookie. *Brilliant.*

Betwixed

1½ C. butter, softened
1 C. powdered sugar
1 tsp. vanilla
3 C. flour
¼ tsp. salt

50 caramels, unwrapped
  (about 1¼ (11 oz.) bags)
1 T. water
1 (11.5 oz.) pkg. milk
  chocolate chips
2 tsp. shortening

Preheat the oven to 350° and line cookie sheets with parchment paper; set aside.

In a medium mixing bowl, beat the butter and powdered sugar until smooth and creamy. Mix in the vanilla, flour, and salt until well blended. Shape dough into two disks and roll out on a lightly floured surface until ½" thick. Cut into rounds with a 2" cookie cutter and arrange on prepped cookie sheets, rerolling the scraps to cut more rounds. Bake 14 to 16 minutes or until just beginning to brown. Let cool.

In a large microwaveable bowl, combine caramels and water. Microwave on high for 2 to 2½ minutes, stirring every minute until smooth. Spread caramel on each cookie, reheating caramel as needed. Let these beauties cool.

Combine the chocolate chips and shortening in another microwaveable bowl and microwave on high for 30 seconds at a time, stirring until melted. Spread chocolate over the cooled caramel and let stand until set. Store at room temperature. *Freezing not recommended.*

Cinnamon Roll Cookies

makes 2½ dozen

Almost like eating a cinnamon roll – but this one's crisp and crunchy. **Delish!**

1 C. plus 6 T. unsalted butter, softened

⅓ C. sugar

1¼ C. powdered sugar, divided

1 tsp. salt, divided

2½ tsp. vanilla, divided

1½ tsp. orange zest

1 egg

2¼ C. plus 2 T. flour, divided

¼ C. light brown sugar

1½ tsp. plus 2 T. light corn syrup, divided

1 T. cinnamon

Water

Directions

In a large mixing bowl, beat together 1 C. butter, sugar, ¾ C. powdered sugar, ½ tsp. salt, 1 tsp. vanilla, and zest on medium speed until light and fluffy, 3 to 4 minutes. Add the egg and beat well. Slowly beat in 2¼ C. flour until just combined. Roll out the dough on a lightly floured surface to make a 12" square. *(A silicone mat or parchment paper works great for this dough.)*

For the filling, beat together the brown sugar, 1½ tsp. corn syrup, cinnamon, ½ tsp. vanilla, and the remaining 6 T. butter, ½ tsp. salt, and 2 T. flour on medium speed for 2 to 3 minutes, until light and fluffy. Spread this cinnamon confection over the dough. Starting at one edge, roll dough into a log shape. Wrap in plastic wrap, pressing gently to make roll even. Freeze at least 20 minutes, until firm *(or refrigerate overnight)*.

To bake the cookies, preheat the oven to 375° and line cookie sheets with parchment paper. Unwrap the dough log and cut into slices, ⅜" thick. Arrange on prepped cookie sheets and bake 12 to 14 minutes or until edges are slightly browned. Let cookies cool a few minutes before removing to a wire rack to finish cooling.

For the glaze, whisk together the remaining ½ C. powdered sugar, 1 tsp. vanilla, and 2 T. corn syrup until smooth, adding up to 1 T. water as needed to make a thin glaze. Brush the glaze over each cookie and let dry. *These freeze best without the glaze.*

Peanutty Chocolate Chippers

Preheat the oven to 350°. In a big mixing bowl, beat together ½ C. each softened butter, shortening, and peanut butter on medium speed about 30 seconds. Add ½ C. sugar, 1 C. light brown sugar, and 1 tsp. baking soda and beat until well combined. Beat in 2 eggs and 1 tsp. vanilla until blended. Slowly beat in 3 C. flour, stirring in the rest with a spoon when dough seems stiff. Stir in ½ C. each semi-sweet and milk chocolate chips, chopped honey roasted peanuts, and bite-size peanut butter cups *(halved)*.

Drop the dough by rounded teaspoonful, 2" apart, onto parchment paper-lined cookie sheets and bake 11 to 14 minutes or until light golden brown. Cool slightly, then remove to a wire rack to cool completely. *These freeze well.*

makes 4 dozen

Chocolate M&M No-Bakes

In a medium saucepan over medium-high heat, melt ½ C. unsalted butter. Stir in ½ C. milk, 2 C. sugar, and ¼ C. unsweetened cocoa powder and bring to a boil; boil for 1 to 2 minutes, stirring frequently. Remove from heat and stir in ½ C. creamy peanut butter *(not reduced fat)* and 1 tsp. vanilla until smooth. Stir in 2½ C. quick oats, 1 C. coarsely chopped pretzel M&Ms, and ¼ tsp. sea salt until combined. Drop the chocolatey good mixture by rounded tablespoonful onto waxed paper and let cool completely until set. *Freezing not recommended.*

Oatmeal Spice Sandwiches

3 C. quick oats, coarsely ground

1½ C. flour

1 tsp. baking soda

Salt

¾ tsp. cinnamon

¼ tsp. ground cloves

1¾ C. unsalted butter, softened, divided

½ C. sugar

1 C. dark brown sugar

1 egg

1 T. molasses

2½ tsp. vanilla, divided

1 (7 oz.) tub marshmallow crème

1 C. powdered sugar

1 (13 oz.) jar Nutella hazelnut spread

Preheat the oven to 375° and line cookie sheets with parchment paper. In a bowl, mix the oats, flour, baking soda, ½ tsp. salt, cinnamon, and cloves; set everything aside.

In a mixing bowl, beat 1¼ C. butter, sugar, and brown sugar on medium speed until light and creamy. Beat in egg, molasses, and 2 tsp. vanilla until blended. Slowly beat in the set-aside oats mixture, stirring in any remainder with a spoon. Drop dough by large spoonful *(2 T. per cookie)* onto prepped cookie sheets, 2" apart. Flatten tops lightly and bake 9 to 12 minutes or until edges are lightly browned. Cool slightly, then remove to a wire rack to finish cooling.

For the filling, beat the remaining ½ C. butter on high speed until creamy; beat in marshmallow crème. Slowly beat in the powdered sugar and remaining ½ tsp. vanilla until fluffy.

Spread some filling on the bottom of half the cookies and Nutella on the bottom of remaining cookies. Sandwich cookies together, filling sides in. *Freezing not recommended.*

Double the fun when a marshmallow crème filling and Nutella are sandwiched between two yummy oatmeal cookies.

11

Chocolate Rolo Rounds

makes 4 dozen

Nothing beats melted caramel goodness baked inside a delicious chocolate cookie – until you drizzle more caramel over the top and add a sprinkling of sea salt. Double the bliss!

2¾ C. flour

¾ C. unsweetened cocoa powder

1 tsp. baking soda

¼ tsp. salt

1 C. butter, softened

1 C. sugar

1 C. light brown sugar

2 eggs

2 tsp. vanilla

48 Rolo chocolate-covered caramels, unwrapped

½ C. caramel bits

1½ to 2 T. heavy cream

Coarse sea salt

Directions

Whisk together the flour, cocoa powder, baking soda, and salt in a bowl and set aside. Beat the butter in a large mixing bowl on medium speed until creamy. Add the sugar and brown sugar and beat until well combined. Beat in the eggs and vanilla, then gradually beat in as much of the set-aside flour mixture as possible, stirring in the rest with a spoon. Cover and chill dough about 1 hour.

To bake the cookies, preheat the oven to 375° and line cookie sheets with parchment paper. Shape dough into 1½" balls, press a Rolo inside each one, and wrap dough around candy to seal it inside. Set on prepped cookie sheets, 2" apart, and bake 8 to 10 minutes or until edges are firm. Cool a few minutes before removing to a wire rack to cool completely.

Meanwhile, combine the caramel bits and cream in a microwaveable bowl and microwave on high for 30 to 40 seconds; stir until melted and smooth. Drizzle the caramel over each cookie and sprinkle with sea salt. Let stand until set. *These freeze well.*

Break it open...
A Rolo candy tucked inside a cookie is pure chocolate-caramel genius!

White Chocolate Macadamia Cookies

Crisp and chewy, sweet and nutty, these cookies will make you swooooon.

- 2 C. plus 2 T. flour
- ½ tsp. baking soda
- ¼ tsp. salt
- ¾ C. unsalted butter, softened
- ½ C. sugar
- 1 C. light brown sugar
- 1 egg plus 1 egg yolk
- 2 tsp. vanilla
- ¾ C. white chocolate chips
- ¾ C. coarsely chopped macadamia nuts

Directions

In a medium bowl, stir together the flour, baking soda, and salt; set aside. In a large mixing bowl, beat the butter, sugar, and brown sugar on medium speed until creamy. Mix in the egg, egg yolk, and vanilla until just combined. Slowly beat in the set-aside flour mixture until well blended. Stir in the chips and nuts; cover and chill the dough at least 1 hour *(or up to 5 days)*.

To bake the cookies, preheat the oven to 350° and line cookie sheets with parchment paper. Drop the dough by rounded tablespoonful onto prepped cookie sheets, about 2" apart. *(Keep dough refrigerated between batches.)* Bake 9 to 12 minutes or until light golden brown. Let cookies cool slightly before removing to a wire rack to cool completely. *These freeze well.*

Chill Out!

Chilling dough in the fridge helps cookies develop more flavor and keep their shape during baking. If you're in a hurry, quick-chill dough in the freezer for ⅓ the time.

For fresh-baked drop cookies anytime, freeze cookie-size scoops of dough until firm, then toss them into a container and keep frozen until a craving hits. Thaw slightly and bake as directed.

Coconut-pecan creaminess perched on a crisp double-chocolate cookie: *heaven!*

16

German Chocolate Drops

1¼ C. flour

⅓ C. unsweetened cocoa powder

1 tsp. baking powder

¼ tsp. salt

¾ C. unsalted butter, softened, divided

¾ C. sugar, divided

¾ C. dark brown sugar

1 egg plus 2 egg yolks, divided

1½ tsp. vanilla, divided

1⅓ C. semi-sweet chocolate chips, divided

½ C. evaporated milk

½ C. sweetened flaked coconut

½ C. chopped pecans

Preheat the oven to 350° and line cookie sheets with parchment paper. In a bowl, whisk together the flour, cocoa powder, baking powder, and salt; set everything aside.

In a mixing bowl, beat ½ C. butter, ¼ C. sugar, and brown sugar on medium-high speed until well mixed. Add the egg, 1 egg yolk, and 1 tsp. vanilla; beat until combined. Slowly beat in the set-aside flour mixture and then stir in 1 C. chocolate chips.

Drop dough by big spoonful onto prepped cookie sheets, 2" apart, and bake 10 to 12 minutes or until set. Cool slightly, then remove to wire racks until cool.

For the toppings, whisk together the milk and remaining ¼ C. butter, ½ C. sugar, and egg yolk in a saucepan over medium heat. Cook and stir often until thickened, about 10 minutes. Remove from heat and stir in coconut, pecans, and remaining ½ tsp. vanilla; let cool to thicken. Spread mixture on cookies. Melt the remaining ⅓ C. chocolate chips and drizzle over cookies. Let cool at least 15 minutes. *Freezing not recommended.*

Date & Raisin Filled Cookies

makes 4 dozen

A touch of citrus glaze on these old-fashioned cookies is an excellent update – sweet and so satisfying!

⅔ C. butter, softened

1⅓ C. plus ½ C. sugar, divided

¾ tsp. vanilla

2 eggs

2⅔ C. flour

¼ tsp. salt

1½ tsp. cornstarch

¼ tsp. cinnamon

1 C. chopped dates

½ C. raisins

½ C. water

½ tsp. orange extract

½ tsp. orange zest

½ C. powdered sugar

Milk

Directions

In a large mixing bowl, beat together the butter and 1⅓ C. sugar on medium speed until creamy. Add the vanilla, then beat in the eggs, one at a time. Gradually beat in flour and salt until well combined. Cover and chill dough for 2 to 3 hours.

In a small saucepan over medium heat, combine the remaining ½ C. sugar, cornstarch, cinnamon, dates, raisins, and water. Cook and stir until bubbly and thickened; let cool.

To bake the cookies, preheat the oven to 400° and line cookie sheets with parchment paper. On a lightly floured surface, roll out half the dough until ⅛" thick. Cut rounds with a 2" cookie cutter and arrange on prepped cookie sheets; reroll the scraps. Spoon a scant 1 tsp. date filling onto the center of each cookie. Roll out remaining dough and cut rounds as before, but cut another hole in the center of each cookie with a 1" cutter. Set "ring" cookies on the rounds with filling and seal the outer edges together with a fork. Bake 10 to 12 minutes, until edges just start to brown. Cool slightly and then remove to wire racks to cool completely. Whisk together the orange extract, zest, powdered sugar, and 2 to 3 tsp. milk to make a thin glaze. Drizzle over cooled cookies. *These freeze best without the glaze.*

In a Hurry?

Skip the extra cutting. Just sandwich the filling between two full cookie rounds and seal the edges together. Sweet little pillows!

Pistachio-Chocolate Crunchers

Place the oven rack in the upper third of the oven and preheat to 300°. Combine 1¼ C. flour, ½ tsp. baking soda, and ¼ tsp. salt in a bowl and set aside.

In a big mixing bowl, beat ½ C. softened unsalted butter, ½ C. sugar, and ½ C. brown sugar on medium speed, 3 to 4 minutes. Add 1 egg and 1 tsp. vanilla and beat well. Slowly beat in the set-aside flour mixture until combined. Stir in 1½ C. dark chocolate chips and 1 C. chopped shelled, roasted, and salted pistachios. Using a 1½" cookie scoop, drop the dough onto parchment paper-lined cookie sheets, about 2" apart. Sprinkle with smoked sea salt and bake 18 to 20 minutes or until golden brown. Cool 5 minutes before removing cookies to a wire rack to finish cooling. *These freeze well.*

makes 2½ dozen

Cran-Orange Shortbread

Place ½ C. dried sweetened cranberries and ¼ C. sugar in a food processor and pulse to chop the berries; dump into a big bowl. Then pulse together ½ C. sugar, 2½ C. flour, and 1 C. cold cubed butter until very fine crumbs form; add to the cranberry mixture. Stir in 1 tsp. almond extract and the zest of 1 orange. Knead dough just until it holds together; shape into a log *(2" in diameter)*, wrap in plastic wrap, and chill at least 2 hours.

To bake the cookies, preheat the oven to 350°. Slice dough into ¼"-thick rounds and coat in sugar, if you'd like. Arrange on parchment paper-lined cookie sheets and bake 12 to 14 minutes or until just starting to brown. Cool slightly, then remove to a wire rack until cool. To add a glaze, mix 1 T. orange juice, ¼ tsp. each orange and almond extracts, and ½ C. powdered sugar and brush it on. *These freeze well.*

Molasses-Ginger Dips

4 tsp. cinnamon, divided

2½ C. sugar, divided

1½ C. vegetable oil

2 eggs

½ C. molasses

4 C. flour

4 tsp. baking soda

1 tsp. salt

1 T. ground ginger

1 (12 oz.) pkg. white chocolate chips

Finely chopped milk chocolate toffee bits

Preheat the oven to 350° and line cookie sheets with parchment paper. Mix 2 tsp. cinnamon and ½ C. sugar in a small bowl and set everything aside.

In a large mixing bowl, beat together the remaining 2 C. sugar, oil, eggs, molasses, flour, baking soda, salt, ginger, and remaining 2 tsp. cinnamon until well combined. Shape dough into balls by rounded teaspoonful and roll in the set-aside sugar mixture to coat. Place on prepped cookie sheets, 3" apart, and bake 8 to 10 minutes. Cool slightly before removing to a wire rack to cool completely.

Place the white chips in a small microwaveable bowl and microwave until melted and smooth, stirring every 15 seconds. Dip cookies into the melted chips to partially coat, letting excess drip off. Set dipped cookies aside for a minute or two before dipping the coated edge into toffee bits; set on waxed paper to dry. *These freeze best before dipping.*

Go beyond ordinary when you ramp up the flavor in these delicious molasses-ginger cookies with white chocolate and toffee bits. **Delectable!**

Sugar Cookie Bars

makes 1½ dozen

No time for cut-out cookies? Get the great flavor of chewy sugar cookies with none of the stress or mess. Perfectly sweet!

2½ C. flour

½ tsp. baking powder

½ tsp. salt

½ C. plus 5 T. butter, softened, divided

1 C. sugar

1 egg

2 T. sour cream

1 tsp. plus 1 T. vanilla, divided

3 to 4 T. heavy cream

4 C. powdered sugar

Food coloring

Candy sprinkles

Directions

Preheat the oven to 375°. Line a 9 x 13" baking pan with foil and coat with cooking spray. In a bowl, whisk together the flour, baking powder, and salt; set everything aside.

In a big mixing bowl, beat ½ C. butter and the sugar together until light and fluffy, about 3 minutes. Add the egg, sour cream, and 1 tsp. vanilla and mix well. Slowly stir in the set-aside flour mixture until combined. Press dough evenly into the prepped pan and bake 15 to 17 minutes or until edges begin to turn golden. Cool completely.

For the frosting, beat together the remaining 5 T. butter, 1 T. vanilla, cream, and powdered sugar until nice and creamy. Stir in food coloring until you get a color you like. Spread over the cookie base and top with your favorite candy sprinkles. Cut into bars to serve. *These freeze best without the sprinkles.*

Choose Your Style

If you like thinner sugar cookies, press the dough into a 10 x 15" jellyroll pan and adjust the baking time as needed.

Thinnish Mints

makes 2½ dozen

Bigger and even better than their famous boxed cousins!

1⅓ C. flour

¾ C. unsweetened cocoa powder

1 tsp. baking powder

⅛ tsp. salt

¾ C. unsalted butter, softened

1 C. sugar

1 egg

1 tsp. vanilla

1¾ tsp. oil-based peppermint extract, divided

1 to 1½ (12 oz.) pkgs. dark chocolate candy melts

Directions

In a bowl, whisk together the flour, cocoa powder, baking powder, and salt; set aside. In a large mixing bowl, beat the butter on medium speed until smooth and creamy. Add the sugar and beat until light and fluffy. Beat in the egg, vanilla, and 1 tsp. peppermint extract until blended. Slowly beat in the set-aside flour mixture until well combined. Divide dough into two even portions and roll each into a log, 2" in diameter. Wrap in plastic wrap and chill several hours.

To bake the cookies, preheat the oven to 350° and line cookie sheets with parchment paper. Unwrap the dough logs and cut into slices about ⅜" thick. Arrange slices on prepped cookie sheets and bake 8 to 10 minutes. Let cool a few minutes before removing to a wire rack to cool completely.

To coat the cookies, melt the candy melts according to the package directions and stir in the remaining ¾ tsp. peppermint extract. Coat each cookie in melted chocolate deliciousness and set on waxed paper, remelting the remaining chocolate as needed for easy coverage. Chill about 15 minutes or until set. Store at room temperature. *Freezing not recommended.*

makes 8½ dozen

3-In-1 Cookies

Prepare one basic dough, divide it in thirds, and customize each portion to create three different types of cookies. It will look like you baked all day – but you didn't!

2½ C. unsalted butter, softened

2 C. sugar

5½ C. flour

1½ tsp. salt

2½ tsp. vanilla

28

Directions

Preheat the oven to 325° and line cookie sheets with parchment paper. Make the base cookie dough by beating the butter in a large mixing bowl on medium speed until creamy. Gradually beat in the sugar, flour, and salt until light and fluffy. Add vanilla and beat about 5 minutes. Divide the dough evenly among three bowls to prepare three different flavors. *These freeze well.*

Peanut Butter

To one bowl of dough, stir in ½ C. creamy peanut butter and ½ C. finely chopped peanuts. Shape dough into balls by rounded teaspoonful, then roll in sugar. Set on prepped cookie sheets and use a fork to flatten lightly in a crisscross pattern. Bake 15 to 18 minutes and cool on a wire rack. *Makes 3½ dozen*

Cherry Pinwheels

To another bowl of dough, mix in ¾ tsp. cherry extract. Roll out dough on a lightly floured surface into a ³⁄₁₆"-thick rectangle *(about 10 x 15")* and spread with ⅓ C. drained, diced maraschino cherries. Starting on one long edge, roll dough into a log and freeze until firm. Cut log into ½"-thick slices and bake on prepped cookie sheets about 20 minutes. Glaze hot cookies with a mixture of 1½ tsp. melted butter, ½ C. powdered sugar, a few drops of cherry extract, and enough milk to make it thin. Let dry on a wire rack. *Makes 2½ dozen*

M&M Favorites

To the last bowl of dough, stir in ½ C. mini M&Ms. Use a cookie scoop to drop dough onto prepped cookie sheets and bake 15 to 18 minutes. Cool on a wire rack. *Makes 2½ dozen*

Bite-size pecan pies with an oh-so-tender cookie crust — not just for holidays!

Pecan Tassies

½ C. unsalted butter, softened

3 oz. cream cheese, softened

1 C. flour

1 T. butter, melted

1 egg

¾ C. light brown sugar

1 tsp. vanilla

Pinch of salt

½ C. chopped pecans

In a medium mixing bowl, combine the softened butter and cream cheese; beat together on medium speed until smooth and creamy. Beat in the flour until combined. Cover and refrigerate dough for 1 hour.

To bake the cookies, preheat the oven to 325° and coat 24 mini muffin cups with cooking spray. Whisk together the melted butter, egg, brown sugar, vanilla, and salt until smooth. Stir in the pecans and set everything aside.

Roll the dough into 1" to 1¼" balls and press each one evenly over the bottom and side of a muffin cup for the crust. Spoon a scant tablespoonful of the pecan mixture into each crust. Bake about 18 minutes or until crust is light brown and filling is puffy and set. Cool in pans for 10 minutes before removing to a wire rack to cool completely. *These freeze well.*

makes 3½ dozen

Raspberry Thumbprints

In a mixing bowl, beat 1 C. softened butter just until smooth and creamy. Beat in ⅔ C. sugar and ½ tsp. almond extract until combined. Gradually beat in 2 C. flour, stirring in any remainder with a spoon. Cover and chill dough for 1 hour.

To bake the cookies, preheat the oven to 350°. Shape dough into 1" balls and place on parchment paper-lined cookie sheets. Press your thumb or a wooden spoon handle into the center of each ball to make a deep dent. Fill dents with red raspberry jam and bake about 10 minutes or until edges are light brown. Cool slightly before removing cookies to a wire rack to cool completely.

For the icing, mix 1 C. powdered sugar, 1½ tsp. almond extract, and 1 or 2 tsp. water. Drizzle over cookies and let dry. *These freeze best before icing.*

makes 3 dozen

Butter Pecan Sandies

Preheat the oven to 350°. Spread 1½ C. chopped pecans on a rimmed baking sheet and toast the nuts about 6 minutes; let cool.

In a mixing bowl, beat 1 C. softened unsalted butter and ⅔ C. sugar until light, about 1 minute. Beat in 2 tsp. vanilla, 2 C. flour, and ¼ tsp. salt until dough comes together. Knead in the pecans. Shape the dough into 1½" balls and roll in more sugar. Arrange on parchment paper-lined cookie sheets and gently flatten with the bottom of a drinking glass. Sprinkle tops with a little more sugar and bake on an upper rack in the oven for 12 to 14 minutes or until bottoms just begin to brown. Cool slightly before removing to a wire rack to finish cooling. Sprinkle with powdered sugar for a nice finishing touch. *These freeze well before sprinkling.*

Sliced Chocolate Swirls

makes 4½ dozen

Deliciously different. Crunchy and satisfying. If you love brown sugar cookies, you'll gobble up these pretty treats.

1 C. semi-sweet chocolate chips

½ C. sweetened condensed milk

1 T. shortening

¾ C. butter, softened

½ tsp. salt

1 tsp. almond extract

¾ C. light brown sugar

2 C. flour

Milk

¾ C. chopped almonds or walnuts

Powdered sugar, optional

Directions

Preheat the oven to 350° and line cookie sheets with parchment paper; set aside. In the top of a double boiler, combine the chocolate chips, condensed milk, and shortening; cook over low heat until melted and smooth, stirring often. Let filling cool slightly.

Meanwhile, put the butter, salt, almond extract, and brown sugar in a large mixing bowl and beat on medium speed until creamy. Mix in the flour, then stir in 2 to 3 tsp. milk as needed until dough holds together. Knead the dough just until smooth and divide into three even portions. On a lightly floured surface, roll out each portion into a 6 x 10" rectangle. Spread ⅓ of the chocolate filling over each rectangle and sprinkle each with ¼ C. almonds. Starting with a long side, roll up the dough and transfer to prepped cookie sheets. Bake 20 to 23 minutes or until light golden brown. Cool slightly before removing to a wire rack. Cool completely and wrap tightly in plastic wrap. To serve, sprinkle with powdered sugar, if you'd like, and slice diagonally, about ⅜" thick. *These freeze well.*

Serve it later...
You can freeze a whole cookie roll after baking – then just defrost and slice for a ready-to-eat treat. Company-worthy, company-ready!

Iced Coconut-Lime Shortbread

A zippy lime kick in a light crunchy cookie – perfect for summer or anytime!

½ C. sweetened flaked coconut

½ C. sugar

2 T. plus 1 tsp. lime zest, divided, plus more for sprinkling

1 tsp. clear vanilla

2½ C. flour

1 C. cold butter, sliced

Water

2 C. powdered sugar

1 T. lime juice

Directions

Preheat the oven to 325° and line cookie sheets with parchment paper; set aside.

In a food processor, combine the coconut, sugar, 2 T. lime zest, and vanilla; pulse until coconut is finely chopped. Add the flour and pulse to combine. Gradually add the butter pieces and pulse until a smooth dry dough forms. Transfer to a large bowl and knead the dough, adding a teaspoon or two of water as needed to make everything hold together. Divide the dough in half and shape each portion into a ball. On a lightly floured surface, roll out each ball of dough until ¼" thick. Cut out rounds with a cookie cutter – make 'em big or small – and place on prepped cookie sheets. Bake 15 to 17 minutes or until bottoms just begin to brown. Cool slightly, then remove to wire racks to cool completely.

For the icing, whisk together the powdered sugar, lime juice, 1 tsp. zest, and just enough water to make a spreading consistency you like. Spread this zippy icing over the cookies and sprinkle with any remaining zest. Let stand until set. *These freeze best without icing.*

Don't limit yourself to apricot preserves. These taste great with blueberry, strawberry, cherry... well, you get the idea.

Apricot Bowties

8 oz. cream cheese, softened

1 C. unsalted butter, softened

½ tsp. vanilla

1 tsp. almond extract

¾ tsp. salt

2½ C. flour

¾ C. apricot preserves

1 egg, beaten

Powdered sugar

In a large mixing bowl, beat the cream cheese and butter on medium speed for 3 minutes, until light and fluffy. Beat in the vanilla and almond extract. Slowly beat in the salt and 2½ C. flour until dough forms, stirring in any remainder with a spoon. On a lightly floured surface, knead the dough a few times to form a smooth ball. Divide dough into thirds, flatten into squares, and wrap each in plastic wrap. Chill at least 4 hours.

To bake the cookies, soften dough at room temperature about 15 minutes. Preheat the oven to 400° and line cookie sheets with parchment paper. Roll out each portion of dough into an 8 x 12" rectangle, ⅛" thick. With a pizza cutter, trim edges and then cut dough into 2" squares; arrange on prepped cookie sheets. Spoon ½ tsp. preserves onto the center of each square. Fold one corner to the center, moisten with beaten egg, then fold opposite corner to the center; press and seal with more egg. Bake 10 to 12 minutes, until lightly browned and puffy. Cool slightly before removing to a wire rack to finish cooling. Sprinkle with powdered sugar, or if you prefer, drizzle with a glaze made by mixing ½ C. powdered sugar with 1 T. liquid amaretto coffee creamer. *These freeze best before sprinkling or glazing.*

Snickering Cookie Bars

makes 2 dozen

With the crunchy goodness of a cookie and the sweet toppings of a candy bar, these treats will earn two thumbs up every time!

⅔ C. butter, softened

¼ C. sugar

1¼ C. flour

¼ tsp. salt

1 tsp. vanilla

1 (11 oz.) bag caramels, unwrapped

¼ C. heavy cream

1 C. dry-roasted peanuts

1 (11.5 oz.) pkg. milk chocolate chips

Directions

Preheat the oven to 350° and line a 9 x 9" baking pan with parchment paper, allowing some to hang over sides of pan; set aside. In a medium mixing bowl, beat the butter on medium speed until creamy. Beat in the sugar, flour, salt, and vanilla until well mixed and crumbly. Press into the prepped pan and bake about 20 minutes or until lightly browned. Let cool.

Combine the caramels and cream in the microwave on high for 30 seconds at a time, stirring until smooth. Stir in the peanuts and spread the mixture evenly over the crust; let cool at least 10 minutes.

In a clean microwaveable bowl, melt the chocolate chips in the microwave for 30 seconds at a time, stirring until smooth. Pour the chocolate over the caramel layer and spread evenly. Let cool about 3 hours or until chocolate looks dry. Lift parchment paper to remove from pan and cut into bars. *(You can pop the pan into the freezer for 5 minutes first to make cutting easy.) Freezing not recommended.*

Peanut Crisps

Tender and crunchy, these old-fashioned peanut cookies will have everyone begging for more!

1 C. margarine, softened
  (not from a tub)

1 C. vegetable oil

1 C. sugar

1 C. brown sugar

1 egg

1 C. quick-cooking oats

1 C. crisp rice cereal

1 tsp. vanilla

½ tsp. salt

3½ C. flour, divided

1 tsp. baking soda

1 tsp. cream of tartar

Salted peanuts, halved

Directions

Preheat the oven to 350° and line cookie sheets with parchment paper; set aside.

In a large mixing bowl, beat the margarine, oil, sugar, brown sugar, and egg on medium speed for 2 or 3 minutes. Add the oats, cereal, vanilla, and salt, beating until well combined. Add 1½ C. flour, baking soda, and cream of tartar and beat well. Slowly beat in as much of the remaining 2 C. flour as possible, stirring in the rest with a spoon if dough gets too stiff. Shape the dough into 1½" balls and place on prepped cookie sheets. Flatten slightly and arrange 4 cute little peanut halves on top of each cookie. Bake about 14 minutes or until lightly browned. Let cookies cool a few minutes before removing to a wire rack to cool completely. *These freeze well.*

Gifting...

These cookies are sturdy enough to stack and pack for successful gift-giving and they freeze well for bake-ahead convenience. Make a bunch to share!

makes 2 dozen

No-Bake Peanut Butter Bites

Line an 8 x 8" pan with foil and spritz with cooking spray; set aside. In a bowl, mix 6 T. melted butter, ½ tsp. vanilla, ⅔ C. creamy peanut butter, 2 C. crisp rice cereal, and 1½ C. powdered sugar. Press mixture into prepped pan and press ¼ C. chopped peanuts into the top. Chill at least 1 hour. Lift foil to remove from pan and cut into squares *(or cut circles with a small cookie cutter)*. Set on waxed paper.

Combine ½ C. 60% cacao bittersweet chocolate chips and 2 T. creamy peanut butter in a microwaveable bowl and microwave on 50% power for 45 seconds. Stir and microwave again in 20 second bursts until melted and smooth. Dip the bottom of each bar *(not the peanut side)* into chocolate, then flip bars chocolate side up and set on waxed paper to dry. Store in the refrigerator. *Freezing not recommended.*

Chippy Puddin' Cookies

Preheat the oven to 350°. Combine 2¼ C. flour, 1 tsp. baking soda, and 2 tsp. baking powder in a bowl and set aside.

In a mixing bowl, beat together ½ C. each softened butter, softened margarine *(not from a tub)*, sugar, and light brown sugar on medium speed until creamy. On low, beat in 1 (3.4 oz.) pkg. vanilla instant pudding mix and 1 tsp. vanilla until combined. Beat in 2 eggs, then slowly beat in the set-aside flour mixture until just blended. Stir in 1 C. each milk chocolate chips and either butterscotch or white chocolate chips. Drop the dough by rounded spoonful or cookie scoop onto parchment paper-lined cookie sheets and bake until lightly browned, 9 to 12 minutes. Cool slightly before removing to a wire rack to cool completely. *These freeze well.*

Glazed Lemon Ricotta Drops

2½ C. flour

1 tsp. baking powder

1 tsp. salt

½ C. unsalted butter, softened

2 C. sugar

2 eggs

1 (15 oz.) tub whole milk ricotta cheese, at room temperature

Zest and juice of 2 lemons, divided

1½ C. powdered sugar

Preheat the oven to 375° and line cookie sheets with parchment paper. In a bowl, whisk together the flour, baking powder, and salt; set everything aside.

In a large mixing bowl, beat the butter and sugar on medium speed for 3 minutes, until light and fluffy. Beat in the eggs, one at a time, until blended. Add the ricotta, 1 T. plus 1 tsp. lemon zest, and 3 T. lemon juice; beat well. Gradually beat in as much of the set-aside flour mixture as possible, stirring in the rest with a spoon. Drop the dough by heaping tablespoonful onto prepped cookie sheets and bake 13 to 15 minutes or until slightly golden around edges. Let cool a few minutes before removing to a wire rack to finish cooling.

For the glaze, whisk together the powdered sugar, remaining lemon zest, and 2 to 2½ T. of the remaining lemon juice until smooth and glaze-like. Spread about ½ tsp. glaze over each cookie and let dry. *These freeze well before glazing.*

These soft lemon cookies are so mouthwatering and light, they'll be gone before you know it!

47

Pumpkin Cheesecake Doodles

makes 2½ dozen

Cheesecake:
delicious.
Snickerdoodles:
yummy.
Pumpkin pie:
divine.
Putting cheesecake
inside a pumpkin-
flavored doodle:
EXTRAORDINARY!

3¾ C. flour

1½ tsp. baking powder

½ tsp. salt

¼ tsp. ground nutmeg

2½ tsp. cinnamon, divided

1 C. unsalted butter, softened

½ C. brown sugar

1¾ C. sugar, divided

1 C. pumpkin puree

1 egg

4 tsp. vanilla, divided

1 (8 oz.) pkg. cream cheese,
softened

1 tsp. ground ginger

⅛ tsp. ground allspice

Directions

Whisk together the flour, baking powder, salt, nutmeg, and ½ tsp. cinnamon in a bowl and set aside. In a mixing bowl, beat together the butter, brown sugar, and 1 C. sugar on medium speed until fluffy, 2 to 3 minutes. Beat in the pumpkin puree, egg, and 2 tsp. vanilla. Slowly beat in the set-aside flour mixture until just combined. Cover and chill dough for 1 hour.

For the filling, beat together the cream cheese, ¼ C. sugar, and remaining 2 tsp. vanilla until blended; cover and chill for 1 hour. For the sugar coating, mix the ginger, allspice, and the remaining 2 tsp. cinnamon and 1 C. sugar in a small bowl; set aside.

To bake the cookies, preheat the oven to 350° and line cookie sheets with parchment paper. Set 1 T. dough into the set-aside sugar coating; flatten dough slightly and turn to coat the other side. Set dough on a prepped cookie sheet and top with 1 tsp. filling. Coat another tablespoonful of dough in the same way and place it over the filling; pinch edges to seal the sweet creamy filling inside, then gently roll into a ball. Roll in sugar coating and return to the cookie sheet. Repeat, spacing cookies 2" apart. *(Keep any remaining cookie dough and filling chilled between batches.)* Bake 15 to 20 minutes or until tops start to crack. Let cool 5 minutes before removing to a wire rack to finish cooling. Store in the refrigerator. *Freezing not recommended.*

Buttery Orange Blossoms

makes 4 dozen

So light and tender, you'll be tempted to eat a whole handful of these sweet blossoms!

½ C. butter, softened, divided

1 C. sugar, divided

¾ tsp. baking soda

¾ tsp. cream of tartar

½ tsp. salt

1 egg

1 tsp. orange zest

½ tsp. vanilla

1 tsp. orange extract, divided

6 T. olive oil

¼ C. white cornmeal

2 C. flour

1 C. powdered sugar

1 T. milk

Food coloring

Directions

In a large mixing bowl, beat 6 T. butter on high speed, just until creamy. Add ¾ C. sugar, baking soda, cream of tartar, and salt and beat together until light and fluffy. Beat in the egg, zest, vanilla, and ½ tsp. orange extract until blended. Gradually beat in the oil until smooth. Mix in the cornmeal and as much of the flour as possible, stirring in the rest with a spoon. Cover and chill dough at least 30 minutes.

To bake the cookies, preheat the oven to 350° and line cookie sheets with parchment paper. Pour the remaining ¼ C. sugar into a small bowl. Shape the dough into 1" balls and roll in the sugar to coat. Arrange on prepped cookie sheets and press an "X" into each ball of dough with a toothpick. Bake 9 to 12 minutes or until tops are very lightly browned. While warm, press cookies with the toothpick again to deepen the creases. Let cool slightly before removing to a wire rack to finish cooling.

For the frosting, whisk together powdered sugar, milk, and the remaining 2 T. butter and ½ tsp. orange extract until smooth and creamy. Stir in food coloring as desired and pipe a dab of frosting in the center of each cookie. *These freeze well.*

How many flavors can you pack into a cookie? You won't believe this flavor explosion — and the turbinado sugar adds a crunchy finish.

52

Chocolate-Chipotle Oatmeal

2 T. unsweetened cocoa powder

1 T. cinnamon

1¼ C. finely ground quick oats

½ C. finely crushed cinnamon graham crackers

¾ C. flour

½ tsp. baking soda

½ tsp. chipotle chili powder

¼ tsp. salt

½ C. butter, softened

¼ C. sugar

1 C. brown sugar

1 egg

¾ tsp. cinnamon extract

½ tsp. vanilla

½ C. cinnamon baking chips

¼ C. mini semi-sweet chocolate chips

1 (1.55 oz.) milk chocolate candy bar, grated

½ oz. unsweetened baking chocolate, finely chopped

Tubinado sugar

Preheat the oven to 350° and line cookie sheets with parchment paper. Whisk together the cocoa powder, cinnamon, oats, cracker crumbs, flour, baking soda, chili powder, and salt. Set everything aside.

In a large mixing bowl, beat together the butter, sugar, and brown sugar until creamy. Add the egg, cinnamon extract, and vanilla and beat well. Slowly beat in the set-aside flour mixture until combined. Stir in the cinnamon chips and chocolate chips along with grated and chopped chocolates. Shape the dough into 1¼" balls and roll in turbinado sugar; arrange on prepped cookie sheets, 2" apart. Bake 12 to 15 minutes or until golden brown, then sprinkle with more sugar, if you'd like. Let cool several minutes before removing to a wire rack to cool completely. *These freeze well.*

Caramel D'Light Bars

makes 1 ½ dozen

Snack outside the cookie box when you bake a fresh batch of these cookie bars. The taste? Even better than the originals. **Delightful!**

1 C. flour

¼ C. sugar

½ C. butter, softened, divided

¼ tsp. vanilla

Water

25 caramels, unwrapped

2 C. sweetened flaked coconut, toasted,* divided

1 C. semi-sweet chocolate chips, divided

1 tsp. shortening, divided

* Toast coconut in a skillet over medium heat until lightly browned; let cool.

Directions

Preheat the oven to 350° and line a 9 x 9" baking pan with parchment paper, allowing some to hang over sides of pan; set aside.

Mix the flour, sugar, 6 T. butter, vanilla, and 1 tsp. water in a bowl until ingredients come together into a ball. Press into the prepped pan and bake for 15 minutes or until edges are lightly browned. Cool completely.

When crust is cool, combine the caramels, 2 T. water, and the remaining 2 T. butter in a small saucepan over low heat and stir until melted. Add 1½ C. of the toasted coconut and stir well. Spread evenly over crust. Sprinkle with the remaining ½ C. coconut and press into the caramel. Let cool about 1 hour.

Lift parchment paper to remove from pan and cut into bars. Melt ¾ C. chocolate chips and ¾ tsp. shortening in a microwaveable bowl in the microwave, stirring every 15 seconds until smooth. Spread about 1 tsp. chocolate over the bottom of each bar and set on parchment paper to dry. Melt the remaining ¼ C. chocolate chips with ¼ tsp. shortening and drizzle over tops of bars; let cool. *Freezing not recommended.*

Pretzel Scotchies

Butterscotch, chocolate & pretzels – a sweet 'n' salty flavor combo that's irresistible!

- 1 C. unsalted butter
- 2¼ C. bread flour
- 1 tsp. salt
- 1 tsp. baking soda
- 1 C. broken pretzel pieces, divided
- ¼ C. sugar
- 1¼ C. dark brown sugar
- 1 egg plus 1 egg yolk
- 2 T. heavy cream or milk
- 1 tsp. vanilla
- ½ C. butterscotch chips
- ½ C. semi-sweet chocolate chunks

Directions

In a medium saucepan over low heat, melt the butter; increase the heat to medium and cook until butter turns golden brown, but doesn't burn *(watch it closely)*. Remove from heat and let cool about 20 minutes. Meanwhile, combine the flour, salt, and baking soda in a bowl and finely crush ½ C. of the pretzels; set everything aside.

Transfer the brown butter to a large mixing bowl and add the sugar and brown sugar; beat on medium speed for 2 to 3 minutes. Beat in the egg and egg yolk until blended. Add the cream and vanilla and beat 2 to 3 minutes more. Gradually beat in the set-aside flour mixture. With a spoon, stir in the butterscotch chips, chocolate chunks, and remaining ½ C. pretzel pieces until evenly combined. Cover and chill dough for 3 hours *(or overnight)*.

To bake the cookies, preheat the oven to 350° and line cookie sheets with parchment paper. Soften the dough at room temperature about 15 minutes. Scoop heaping tablespoons of dough into rough ball shapes and roll lightly in the set-aside crushed pretzels. Place 2" apart on prepped cookie sheets and bake 10 to 13 minutes or until golden brown. Let cool 5 minutes before removing to a wire rack to cool completely. *These freeze well.*

Cookie Hack!
A neat trick to make drop cookies prettier is to break the scooped dough in half and reshape it slightly, forcing the glorious chips and pretzels to the top.

Cream Wafers

makes 3 dozen

Sweet buttercream frosting between two light and flaky wafer cookies – any color, any flavor, party-perfect!

1¼ C. butter, softened, divided

⅓ C. heavy cream

2 C. flour

¼ C. sugar

1½ C. powdered sugar, sifted

2 tsp. lemon flavoring

2 tsp. lemon zest

Milk or lemon juice, optional

Food coloring, optional

Directions

In a mixing bowl with a paddle beater, combine
1 C. butter, cream, and flour, beating on low speed
until well mixed. Divide dough into three even portions,
flatten slightly, and wrap each in plastic wrap; refrigerate
for 2 hours or until firm.

To bake the cookies, preheat the oven to 375° and line
cookie sheets with parchment paper. On a lightly floured
surface, roll out one portion of dough until 3/16" to
1/4" thick and cut circles with a 1½" round cookie cutter,
rerolling scraps; repeat with remaining dough. Pour the
sugar into a bowl and coat both sides of cookies with
sugar. Arrange on prepped pans and make fork holes in
each one. Bake 7 to 10 minutes or until puffy and slightly
firm, but not browned. Cool briefly before removing to
waxed paper to finish cooling.

For the filling, mix the remaining 1/4 C. butter, powdered
sugar, lemon flavoring, and zest, adding a little milk
or juice if needed to make a thick frosting. Stir in food
coloring as desired. Spread about 1 tsp. frosting between
each pair of cookies. *These freeze well.*

Flavor Variations

Raspberry-Lemon: Use raspberry flavoring instead
of lemon flavoring and stir in the lemon zest.

Toasted Coconut: Use coconut flavoring instead
of lemon flavoring, omit the lemon zest, and stir in
1½ T. toasted coconut.

Coconut-Rum: Use rum flavoring instead of lemon
flavoring, omit the lemon zest, and stir in 1½ T. toasted
coconut. Mmm... tropical paradise!

Brownie Buckeye Cookies

makes 2 dozen

rich fudge brownie
+
peanut butter buckeye
+
chocolate topping =

guilty pleasure!

Better make plenty of these – they'll disappear fast!

1 C. powdered sugar

1 C. creamy peanut butter

1 (18.3 oz.) pkg. fudge brownie mix

¼ C. butter, melted

4 oz. cream cheese, softened

1 egg

4 oz. chocolate candy coating

Directions

Preheat the oven to 350° and line cookie sheets with parchment paper. In a small bowl, mix the powdered sugar and peanut butter until well blended. Shape the mixture into 24 (1") balls. Set everything aside.

In a medium mixing bowl, beat together the brownie mix, butter, cream cheese, and egg on low speed until a dough forms. Drop dough by heaping tablespoonful onto prepped cookie sheets to make 24 round cookies. Bake 12 minutes, until tops are dry and slightly cracked.

As soon as cookies come out of the oven, lightly press a yummy set-aside peanut butter ball into the center of each one. Let cookies cool 5 minutes before removing to a wire rack to finish cooling.

Follow package directions to melt the candy coating in the microwave until smooth. Spoon a little melted chocolate over the peanut butter ball on each cookie. Let stand at room temperature until chocolate is set. *Freezing not recommended.*

Smart Baking

For chewier drop cookies of any kind, remove them from the oven while centers are still a little soft, then let cookies set up and "finish" baking on the pan a few minutes before removing to a wire rack.

Cheerio No-Bakes

In a large saucepan over medium heat, melt 2 T. butter. Add 1 (10 oz.) pkg. mini marshmallows and stir until melted. Remove from the heat and stir in ½ C. crunchy peanut butter *(not reduced fat)*. Then stir in 5 C. Honey Nut Cheerios until completely coated. Carefully fold in ¾ C. peanut butter M&Ms. Use an ice cream scoop to drop the mixture onto parchment paper and let cool. *Freezing not recommended.*

What's in a cookie?
Get the kind you *Really Love!*

Apricot Bowties p.38

Light & Tender

Look for plenty of butter and sometimes added dairy products like sour cream, cream cheese, or heavy cream. Handle the dough gently without over-mixing.

Pistachio-Chocolate p.20

Thin & Crisp

Look for baking soda and lots of granulated sugar and butter. Use drop dough at room temperature; roll out or slice chilled dough very thin. Slightly over-bake and use insulated cookie sheets for more spread.

Lemon Ricotta p.46

Soft & Cake-like

Look for extra eggs or egg whites, baking powder, and/or cake flour for extra rise and less spread. Beat the butter or shortening until light and fluffy.

Molasses-Ginger p.22

Dense & Chewy

Look for things like dark brown sugar, honey, molasses, corn syrup, bread flour, extra egg yolk, melted butter, and/or vegetable oil. Slightly under-bake these cookies.

Remember

Your oven, mixing methods, cookie sheets, and baking times will influence the end results. Experiment until your cookies are just the way you want them, inside and out!

Index